From darkness to light

Words of comfort in times of suffering

To

....

From

....

Jarrold Colour Publications, Norwich.

Aonach Dubh, the 'Black Heights' – dramatic Highland beauty at Glen Coe

Acknowledgements

Scripture quotations from *Good News Bible*, 1976, the Bible Societies and Collins, © American Bible Society. Prayers on pages 7, 18 and 34 are from *The Edge of Glory* © 1985, David Adam, Triangle/SPCK. Poem extracts on pages 51 and 59 are from *Many Voices, One Voice: meditations and prayers*, Eddie Askew, Leprosy Mission. Every effort has been made to trace and acknowledge ownership of copyright; however, copyright has in some cases proved untraceable

Darkness

'It feels as if there's a huge grey blanket over me. I'm weighed down by sadness and gloom, with no light anywhere. It's just darkness on all sides. Everything looks so hopeless and as soon as anyone asks me how I'm really feeling I burst into tears. I feel so stupid.'

Lord, it is dark.
Lord, are you here in my darkness?
Your light has gone out, and so has its reflection
  on men and on all things around me.
Everything seems grey and sombre as when a fog blots
  out the sun and enshrouds the earth.

Michel Quoist

This medieval stone bridge straddles the River Nith at Dumfries

Dejection

'It's more than twelve years now since my husband went off with another woman, and I haven't seen him since. I still feel so rejected and cast aside, and I wonder if I shall ever get over it. Life seems one long struggle.'

> *Day and night I cry, and tears are my only food;*
> *all the time my enemies ask me 'Where is your God?'*
>
> Psalm 42:3

> *Does the road wind uphill all the way?*
> *Yes, to the very end.*
> *Will the day's journey take the whole long day?*
> *From morn to night, my friend.*
> *Shall I find comfort, travel-sore and weak?*
> *Of labour you shall find the sum.*
> *Will there be beds for all who seek?*
> *Yea, beds for all who come.*
>
> *Christina G Rossetti*

Taking a stroll round Frogmore, Berkshire

Fishing boats wait at Crail, Fife

Guilt

'While my mother was dying of cancer and I nursed her for weeks on end we never acknowledged between us what was happening to her. Now I feel so guilty that we didn't communicate at all about what was really going on.'

My sins, O God, are not hidden from you; you know how foolish I have been.

Psalm 69:5

Christ in forgiveness to me be near
Christ in forgiveness come appear
Christ in forgiveness drive off the foe
Christ in forgiveness help me below
Christ in forgiveness give me release
Christ in forgiveness I need thy peace.

David Adam

The quiet charm of Polperro in Cornwall

Sadness

'A year ago my precious little granddaughter was killed by a wild driver. I simply can't forget it, and I wonder where God is in all the sadness in the world. Doesn't he care?'

> *Wake up, Lord! Why are you asleep? Rouse yourself!*
> *Don't reject us for ever! Why are you hiding from us?*
> *Don't forget our suffering and trouble!*
>
> Psalm 44:23-24

> *Lead, kindly light, amid the encircling gloom,*
> *Lead thou me on.*
> *The night is dark, and I am far from home,*
> *Lead thou me on.*
> *Keep thou my feet; I do not ask to see*
> *The distant scene; one step enough for me.*
>
> *Cardinal J H Newman*

French Marigolds – a burst of colour in many summer gardens

The exquisite *Chaenomeles Speciosa* – Japanese quince / Japonica

The River Wye tumbles over rocks at Monsal Dale, Derbyshire

Helplessness

'Looking back at my life, it seems I've often had no real control over what's happened. I've missed so many chances but I feel quite helpless to change things now. A friend said to me 'you know, every day is a new beginning' , and I wish I could believe it's not too late for me.'

That is the mystery of grace:
it never comes too late.
Francois Mauriac

Tell everyone who is discouraged,
'Be strong and don't be afraid. God is coming to your rescue'.
Isaiah 35:4

So o'er the hills of life,
Stormy, forlorn,
Out of the cloud and strife
Sunrise is born;
Swift grows the light for us;
Ended is night for us;
Soundless and bright for us
Breaketh God's morn.
Jan Struther

Loneliness

'Since my husband died six years ago I feel so terribly lonely. Weekends are the worst, when I see families out and about together. That makes me feel more alone than ever.'

My God, my God, why have you abandoned me?
I have cried desperately for help,
but still it does not come.

Psalm 22:1

Abide with me; fast falls the eventide;
The darkness deepens; Lord with me abide:
When other helpers fail, and comforts flee,
Help of the helpless, O abide with me.

H F Lyte

Waters ripple gently near Brownsea Island, Dorset

Boats at work and at play at Ramsgate's Royal Harbour

Worry

'My son has left his wife and children to go and live with their best friend. I can't understand what made him do it and I feel I must have been a dreadful mother who brought him up to behave like this. And I worry so much about my daughter-in-law and her young family.'

Hear my prayer, Lord,
and listen to my cry;
come to my aid when I weep.

Psalm 39:12

Be our strength in hours of weakness,
In our wanderings be our guide;
Through endeavour, failure, danger,
Father, be thou at our side.

L M Willis

A profusion of roses, Spalding, Lincolnshire

The hollyhock has long been a favourite in British cottage gardens

Hatred

'My elderly mother is very demanding and I feel trapped having to care for her night and day. It really gets me down and I long for release. She doesn't understand at all what I'm going through and I feel so resentful. Sometimes I really feel I hate her.'

God be in my head
And in my understanding;
God be in my eyes
And in my looking;
God be in my mouth
And in my speaking;
God be in my heart
And in my thinking;
God be at my end
And at my departing.

Anon

A delightful spot on the Forest Trail
in Glen Coe

Withdrawal

'This morning I can't bring myself to get out of bed. There seems no point in life, so I am covering my head with the bedclothes as I feel it's going to be a dreadful day in every way. All I want to do is withdraw from the world and everybody in it.'

Good shepherd,
 be over me to shelter me
 under me to uphold me
 behind me to direct me
 before me to lead me
 about me to protect me
 ever with me to save me
 above me to lift me
And bring me to the green pastures of
 eternal life.

David Adam

The unspoilt village of North Bovey on the edge of Dartmoor, Devon

Bluebells and azaleas make a stunning impact in Spring

This charming cottage is situated in Bignor, Sussex

Fear

'Today I feel as if I'm sinking below the waters, drawn by some inexplicable force from below. I'm starting to panic because there's no real reason why I should feel like this. I'm so afraid.'

I waited patiently for the Lord's help;
  then he listened to me and heard my cry.
He pulled me out of a dangerous pit,
  out of the deadly quicksand.
He set me safely on a rock
  and made me secure.

Psalm 40:1-2

Guide me, O thou great Redeemer,
  Pilgrim through this barren land;
I am weak, but thou art mighty;
  Hold me with thy powerful hand;
  Bread of heaven,
Feed me now and evermore.

W Williams

Gloom

'I can't bear to watch television, particularly the news, because I identify so strongly with the people going through these terrible experiences. I just have to switch if off or go into another room on my own. It fills me with gloom even to look at the newspaper headlines. Life seems so awful.'

The danger of death was all around me;
*   the waves of destruction rolled over me.*
In my trouble I called to the Lord;
*   I called to my God for help.*
In his temple he heard my voice;
*   he listened to my cry for help.*

Psalm 18:4,6

Can a woman's tender care
Cease towards the child she bare?
Yes, she may forgetful be,
Yet will I remember thee.

W Cowper

The splendour of Balmoral Castle, Grampian

The wide Blackwater estuary makes Maldon, Essex, a popular base for fishing and yachting

Exhaustion

'The phone is ringing but I can't move to answer it in case somebody is making demands on me that I can't meet. I just don't want to be leaned on any more and am utterly exhausted. Someone else will have to take the call, or maybe I'll simply leave it to ring.'

I am worn out, O Lord; have pity on me!
Give me strength; I am completely exhausted.

Psalm 6:2

Come to me, all of you who are tired from carrying heavy loads,
and I will give you rest.

Matthew 11:28

Tranquil beauty at Loch Venacher in the Trossachs, Central

Uselessness

'There's a party this evening but I can't face going. I feel such bad company and so useless. I don't want to meet anybody as I don't think I shall have anything worth saying.'

I am overcome by sorrow;
strengthen me as you have promised.

Psalm 119:28

When by fear my heart is daunted
Thou dost hold me in thy hand;
Prayerless, anxious, vainly haunted,
Thou dost make my courage stand.
Foolish worries, fretting troubles
Melt away at thy command.

P Dearmer

Cotswold charm – the Swan Hotel at Bibury

Tudor houses line Church Lane, Ledbury, Hereford & Worcestershire

A magnificent half-timbered cottage at Gretton, Gloucestershire

Indecision

'Even simple things defeat me. It's my sister's birthday and I wanted to buy her a scarf. It took all my courage to get into the shop, and then I couldn't decide for ages which one to choose. As soon as I left the shop I knew I'd made a mistake, but nothing would make me go back and face the shop assistant again. What agony.'

Saviour, breathe forgiveness o'er us:
All our weakness thou dost know;
Thou didst tread this earth before us,
Thou didst feel its keenest woe;
Lone and dreary, faint and weary,
Through the desert thou didst go.

J Edmeston

The restored 15th century castle at Herstmonceux, Sussex

Desolation

'One day recently I felt that even my closest friends hated me. It was silly because in my heart I know that they care, but I just felt they couldn't possibly like me as I was so horrible. And I thought that God must have given up on me too.'

You have caused my friends to abandon me;
you have made me repulsive to them.

Psalm 88:8

If God is for us, who can be against us?

Romans 8:31

For I am certain that . . . there is nothing in all creation
that will ever be able to separate us from the love of God
which is ours through Christ Jesus our Lord.

Romans 8:38,39

The oast house at Beltring, Kent

Camellia offer a welcome blush of colour in early Spring

Discord

'Whatever my husband does is wrong. If he makes a fuss of me I don't want him, if he ignores me I feel upset. First I want to be left alone, and then I wish he'd come and comfort me. I'm so on edge, the poor man doesn't know what to do for the best.'

God is love: and he enfoldeth
all the world in one embrace;
With unfailing grasp he holdeth
every child of every race.
And when human hearts are breaking
under sorrow's iron rod,
Then they find the self-same aching
deep within the heart of God.

Timothy Rees

Springfields, Spalding – 30 colour-splashed acres of spring flowers and roses

Heaviness

'We went for a country walk by a golden cornfield this evening. It was perfect, but the beauty and colour meant nothing to me as I was completely caught up in my own web of misery.'

Lord from this world's stormy sea
Give your hand for lifting me
Lord lift me from the darkest night
Lord lift me into the realm of light
Lord lift me from this body's pain
Lord lift me up and keep me sane
Lord lift me from the things I dread
Lord lift me from the living dead
Lord lift me from the place I lie
Lord lift me that I never die.

David Adam

The Island of Iona

Acroclinium – everlasting flowers of stunning beauty

Despair

'This afternoon I reached rock bottom. I wanted to walk under the nearest bus and felt there was no future for me at all. I am really in the pits and can't get any lower.'

I have never thought that a Christian would be free of suffering. For our Lord suffered. And I have come to believe that he suffered, not to save us from suffering, but to teach us how to bear suffering. For he knew that there is no life without suffering.

Alan Paton
Cry the Beloved Country

The world will make you suffer.
But be brave! I have defeated the world.

John 16:33

Imposing Stonyhurst College stands near Clitheroe, Lancashire

Glimmer

'Our G.P. is wonderful. He keeps coming regularly and always says, 'It will pass'. Now at last I'm beginning to believe him and see a glimmer of hope. The tablets he gave me have counteracted my weakness and I feel certain that they have helped me start to get on top of things again.'

He said not, 'Thou shalt not be tempested, thou shalt not be travailed, thou shalt not be dis-eased', but he said, 'Thou shalt not be overcome'.

Julian of Norwich

All things pass
God never changes
Patience attains
All that it strives for.
St Theresa's bookmark

An impressive view of Watermouth Castle near Ilfracombe, Devon

Chugging through St John's Lock on the Thames at Lechlade, Gloucestershire

Wintry Broadland scene at Horning, Norfolk

Determination

'I'm determined to get better and back to normal, so I'll put a bold face on it and pretend that I'm O.K. I'll make an effort to go through the motions anyway, and maybe that will help.'

My future is in your hands. How wonderful are your gifts to me: how good they are!

Psalm 16:5,6

I slept and dreamed that life was joy;
I awoke and saw that life was duty;
I acted, and behold: duty was joy.

Tagore

Peace and quiet at Horninghold, Leicestershire

Hope

'Things start to look a bit more hopeful today. I felt able to go out to the shops without panicking, and I was actually quite pleased to see some familiar friendly faces.'

What then can I hope for, Lord?
I put my hope in you.

Psalm 39:7

Let your hope keep you joyful, be patient in your troubles,
and pray at all times.

Romans 12:12

Hope is the thing with feathers on
That perches in the soul
And sings the tune without the words,
And never stops at all.
And sweetest in the gale is heard . . .

Emily Dickinson

A thatcher at work on a cottage at Lyndhurst, Hampshire

Dramatic coastline at Land's End, Cornwall

Acceptance

'It's a lovely feeling to know that I am completely accepted by those closest to me. Even though I feel myself so horrible to be with, I still know that they are prepared to put up with me and accept me, warts and all. I'm beginning to realise that God does, too.'

I wait patiently for God to save me;
I depend on him alone.
He alone protects and saves me;
He is my defender, and I shall never be defeated.

Psalm 62:1,6

Love is patient and kind . . . Love does not keep a record of wrongs . . . Love never gives up; and its faith, hope, and patience never fail.

1 Corinthians 13:4,5,7

Calm waters at Cockwood near Dawlish, Devon

Patience

'My husband's patience is amazing. How he puts up with me I shall never know, as my behaviour must often drive him to distraction. Often he will simply sit quietly and squeeze my hand, and I am so thankful for his concern.'

The Lord gives strength to his people and blesses them with peace.

Psalm 29:11

Drop thy still dews of quietness,
Till all our strivings cease;
Take from our souls the strain and stress,
And let our ordered lives confess
The beauty of thy peace.

J G Whittier

The famous harbour at Lyme Regis, Dorset

Mellow old houses line the Thames at Abingdon, Oxfordshire

Love

'This evening I felt wrapped around by love, the love of my family and friends, and the love of God. I am just resting in that and trying not to be anxious any more. I am now able to trust that all will be well in the end.'

Life is great! – whatever happens,
snow or sunshine, joy or pain,
hardship, grief or disillusion,
suffering that I can't explain –
life is great if someone loves me,
holds my hand and calls my name.

Brian A Wren

Castleton, in the heart of the Peak District

Deer graze peacefully at Wollaton Park, Nottinghamshire

Peace

'Having felt ill at ease with life for so long, today I somehow sensed a peace creeping over me. It's been a time of trauma for us all as a family, but now I begin to feel a quiet peace coming through again. How thankful I am.'

> *When I lie down, I go to sleep in peace;*
> *   you alone, O Lord, keep me perfectly safe.*
>
> Psalm 4:8

> *I put myself in your hand.*
> *The sea is vast. No landmarks.*
> *I don't know the way.*
> *At times I can't even point to north.*
> *Or where the sun sets, hidden by cloud.*
> *But I'm content*
> *to leave the navigation to you.*
> *To meet the unknown.*
> *To find, if not new continents of faith,*
> *at least an island or two.*
> *Knowing that, in spite of storm strength,*
> *all shall be well.*
>
> *Eddie Askew*

Understanding

'Yesterday I had a really useful session with the counsellor I am seeing each week. It's marvellous to be able to talk so freely and in confidence, and I feel greatly strengthened by her sensitivity and understanding.'

In all things God works for good with those who love him.

Romans 8:28

The Lord's my shepherd, I'll not want;
He makes me down to lie
In pastures green, he leadeth me
The quiet waters by.

Francis Rous

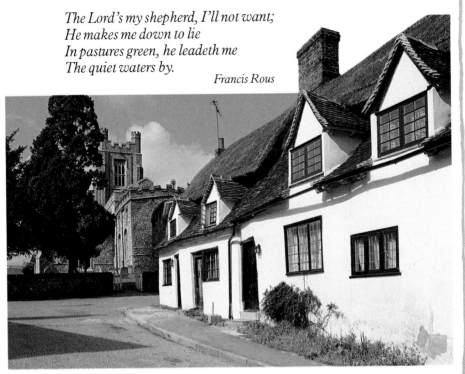

Traditional cottages at Newport, Essex

Mesembryanthemums –
daisy-like blooms in brilliant shades

The chrysanthemum 'Pinnochio' – a dazzling profusion of colour

Concern

'A friend called round to see me today and it certainly cheered me to see her. Somehow she knew instinctively when to talk and when to listen, and when we could just sit in silence together. She brought some lovely flowers and I was so touched by her quiet concern.'

Give praise to the Lord; he has heard my cry for help.
The Lord protects and defends me; I put my trust in him.

Psalm 28:6,7

For the joy of human love,
Brother, sister, parent, child,
Friends on earth, and friends above,
For all gentle thoughts and mild;
Father, unto thee we raise
This our sacrifice of praise.

F S Pierpoint

A glorious sunset at Kyle of Tongue, Highland

Support

"No matter what you do, God still loves you," was the reassuring remark. After all this time I can now begin to feel that God has in fact been carrying me throughout this hellish experience.'

You answered me when I called to you;
with your strength you have strengthened me.
Complete the work that you have begun.

Psalm 138:3,8

Jesu, lover of my soul,
Let me to thy bosom fly,
While the nearer waters roll,
While the tempest still is high;
Hide me, O my Saviour, hide,
Till the storm of life is past;
Safe into the haven guide,
O receive my soul at last.

Charles Wesley

Spectacular Broadland sunset at Hickling, Norfolk

Loch Achray in Central Region, Scotland, is the setting for this stunning Autumn scene

The magnificent harbour at St Peter Port, Guernsey

Calm

'Now I can see that I am sailing into calmer waters. My little boat has been tossed by the waves for long enough, and I do believe that I am coming into harbour at last. A welcome sight indeed.'

He calmed the raging storm, and the waves became quiet.
They were glad because of the calm, and he brought them
safe to the port they wanted.

Psalm 107:29,30

Lord, you are the still centre
of every storm.
In you is calm,
whatever the wind outside.
In you is reassurance,
however high the waves.
In you is strength,
however contrary the tide.

Eddie Askew

Casting cares to the wind at Ambleside in the Lake District

Worth

'Today I actually felt useful for the first time in ages. A friend needed to talk about a problem. All I did was listen but she seemed so grateful for my support. I realised that I am valued as a friend and it felt good to be needed!'

Teach me to feel another's woe
To hide the fault I see
The mercy I to others show
That mercy show to me.

Alexander Pope

Help us to help each other, Lord,
Each other's cross to bear,
Let each his friendly aid afford
And feel his brother's care.

Charles Wesley

Off the beaten track at Kyles Scalpay, near the Isle of Harris

A new day begins in Tobermory on the Island of Mull

Harmony

'This morning when I woke I realised that I was actually better. I know that bad days will come again from time to time, but just at the moment I feel in harmony with myself and with the world. I feel a great sense of relief and thankfulness to be a normal person, and no longer at odds with myself and everyone around me.'

A brighter dawn is breaking,
And earth with praise is waking;
For thou, O King most highest,
The power of death defiest.

In sickness give us healing,
In doubt thy clear revealing,
That praise to thee be given
In earth as in thy heaven.

EH

The imposing Braes of Balquhidder look down on Loch Voil in the Central Region of Scotland

Light

'At last I feel my world is light again. The long dark tunnel seemed endless, but gradually a pinprick appeared and bit by bit I have emerged, with the help of all sorts of people. It's certainly a wonderful feeling, and almost worth all the pain that has gone before.'

God, who has called you out of darkness into his own marvellous light.

1 Peter 2:9

Cometh sunshine after rain,
After sorrow joy again;
After storms of bitter grief
Dawneth God's own sure relief:
And my soul, who from her height
Sank to realms of darkest night,
Wingeth up to heaven her flight.

P Gerhardt, Tr. C Winkworth

A spectacular sunset at Fort George, Highland

ISBN 0-7117-0415-5 © Copyright Jarrold Colour Publications 1989.
Designed and Produced by Parke Sutton Limited, Norwich
for Jarrold Colour Publications, Norwich
Origination by Hilo Offset Ltd. Printed in Portugal